THIS JOURNAL BELONGS TO:

www.ingramcontent.com/pod-product-compliance
Lightning Source LLC
Chambersburg PA
CBHW070436180526
45158CB00018B/1390